...and they two shall BECOME ONE

A SPIRIT SET FREE

INEZ SCRACE

Copyright © 2014 by Inez Scrace

. . . and they two shall become one
a spirit set free
by Inez Scrace

Printed in the United States of America

ISBN 9781498415743

All rights reserved solely by the author. The author guarantees all contents are original and do not infringe upon the legal rights of any other person or work. No part of this book may be reproduced in any form without the permission of the author. The views expressed in this book are not necessarily those of the publisher.

Scripture quotations taken from the King James Version (KJV) – public domain

Scripture quotations taken from The New Strong's Exhaustive Concordance Of The Bible, James Strong, LL.D.,STD by Thomas Nelson Publishers Copyright © 1990. Used by permission. All rights reserved.

Scripture quotations taken from Webster's II New Riverside University Dictionary Copyright © 1984. Used by permission. All rights reserved.

www.xulonpress.com

TABLE OF CONTENTS

Chapter 1. 17

Chapter 2. 25

Chapter 3. 58

Chapter 4. 69

Chapter 5. 80

Every wise woman buildeth her house: but the foolish plucketh it down with her hands.
(Proverbs 14:1 KJV)

INTRODUCTION

"Thus saith the Lord, The heaven is my throne, and the earth is my foot stool: where is the house that ye build unto me? And where is the place of my rest?" (Isaiah 66:1, KJV).

I have lived at my current residence for twenty-five years. Until fifteen years ago I had never been dissatisfied with my house or its furnishings, nor had I thought about changing things around the house. I don't know if it was because making changes wasn't an option for me; early in my marriage I had learned we had no "now" money – only money to be saved for the future. My husband has always been a good steward of money. Our bills are always paid, our credit cards paid in full when due. Whenever we had extra money in the checking account or an income tax refund, it went immediately into some investment for the future, leaving me no time to consider using it. It was never to be seen again.

Even our house was paid off after living in it for only five years. So I never complained. I was truly content because I had what I needed.

Fifteen years ago, though, I began to desire changes in every room. It was as if someone had removed a veil from my eyes. At first I thought it was because I was too busy raising my children to see how outdated and worn everything was around me. But these eyes weren't just opened; they now had magnifying glasses attached, revealing every imperfect inch and corner of the house.

Introduction

First I became dissatisfied with my curtains, which should have been dealt with the moment we moved in. They were thick, beige drapes that could never be free of wrinkles and had rust stains down the sides. I don't know how the rust got there because the drapes came with the house. Next I looked with doubt at the carpet. Soon I wanted new furniture and each room repainted. Eventually I became discontent with everything in every room. I had the hives of discontentment.

I knew accomplishing these changes was an impossible dream because of the lesson I learned early in my marriage. We had what we needed even if some of the furniture pieces were replicas of the furniture in Henry Ford's house, and I'm talking about the museum in Dearborn, Michigan. I know this sounds far fetched, but it's true. One day in 1993 a close friend and I took our children to the Henry Ford Museum. While we strolled along my friend stopped and pointed at the furniture in a display case. "Inez, isn't that the same furniture you have in your house?" my friend asked. I turned, and behind the glass case I saw my couch, my tables and my lamp. We had never laughed so hard. To this day when we think about it we still have a good laugh.

Now you understand my situation and why making these changes was needed yet impossible to fulfill. It was overwhelming to think of the changes I now wanted and desperately needed to make.

I'm not trying to bash my husband. He is a wonderful person and a great provider. We work pretty well together because neither of us is materialistic. If my needs are met I'm content. My family means more to me than stuff. That's why I was so disturbed when I started caring about having everything new. I wouldn't trade my husband for anything in this world.

Introduction

If I could pick someone to marry all over again I would choose him.

I share all this to paint a picture, and even though it's a true picture it is in no way intended to discredit my husband, but rather to help you see how faithful our God is.

I was with another friend of mine one day. She had to go to a home improvement store to pick up something and asked if I wanted to go along. She could do anything she wanted to do to her house and did it without starting world war III. Her husband never said a word; so she often tried to convince me I had the right to do the same. She is a true handywoman; she could build a stone fireplace, lay a ceramic tile floor, install stair rails make stained glass, sew, can, garden, shingle a roof and much more. I had known her only a short while, but we clicked right away. You will find out later how God strategically placed her in my life.

...and they two shall become one

On our way home she suggested we stop at a carpet store. She told me they had a good sale and that I should buy some without my husband's permission. She loved saving money, and it probably was a good sale. Even if I was free to make my own purchases, buying carpet was too big of an item for me not to consult my husband first. He wouldn't buy anything that huge without counsulting with me either.

My carpet was outdated; it looked as if it had been laid when the house was built in 1960. But I did have carpet. It was Berber, so, clean looked dirty, and dirty looked clean. As we browsed through the store the salesman came up to us and asked if we needed help. My friend said yes then asked, "Do you have carpet with a lifetime guarantee? I mean a human lifetime because she, "pointing to me," needs carpet, and if she ever gets any it would be a one-time deal. She will never be able to buy carpet again, so it has to go

Introduction

the distance." Even though the three of us got a laugh out of it, my friend wasn't making fun of me; she was serious and was speaking the truth. The salesman said he didn't have that type of warranty on carpet of course. We thanked him for his time and left.

I have never had a love for the outdoors. To me it's a different world, and I like the one I dwell in more. Indoors. I would probably never go out if I didn't have places to go. Even in the summertime I like being inside. I love having flowers around the outside of the house, but once I plant them I don't go outdoors enough to see that they need watering. So their long lives are attributed to my husband. If it were not for my faithful husband who eventually waters them they would have no hope. He would say to me year after year that if I plant flowers I need to water them to keep them alive.

. . . and they two shall become one

I like being on the inside looking out. I know you might be thinking that maybe I should have been on the outside looking in and then would have noticed the renovation needs. But I don't think that would have made a difference because I was content until now.

As the days continued my "sanctuary" became more and more undesirable. I began spending more time in that foreign land called "outdoors" to avoid facing dreams and desires that meant nothing except they were dreams and desires. I felt sorry for myself and tried to justify why I deserved to have the changes I wanted in my home. But feeling sorry for myself changed nothing.

My heart literally ached as this new interior designer came alive within me. The desire for changes increased, and so did my tears. I was overwhelmed with sadness over the furnishings of my house. Who was this person inside of me? I spent more time in

Introduction

prayer with attempts to cast these troubling thoughts upon the Lord. I felt lost and just wanted to go back to being content with my surroundings, loving my husband and loving my children.

I was frustrated that my mind was filled with thoughts other than those of the Lord and the things of God. These desires were unusual, they were intense, and they were ridiculous to me. I had a nice home – furnishings that were a bit outdated – but a home.

I was in my prayer closet every chance I got. I fasted, worshipped, agonized and asked for forgiveness repeatedly for making the desire for changes to my home an idol.

One day while I was dusting I cried out to the Lord to help me fix up my house so that the pain would go away. The Lord spoke to me and said, "Fix up My house," and this Scripture verse dropped into my spirit: "Thus saith the Lord, The heaven is my throne, and the earth is my foot stool: where is the house that ye build unto me? And where is the place of my rest?" (Isaiah 66:1, KJV). I then realized that God had placed these desires within me so I could seek Him to discover there was more to my Christian walk and marriage than I understood.

He then began to show me the condition of His house within my heart, how He wanted it to look and what I had to do to make the changes He desired. The revelation God placed in my heart has become the basis for writing this book.

CHAPTER 1

"...for the Lord seeth not as man seeth; for man looketh on the outward appearance, but the Lord looketh on the heart. (1 Sam 16:7 KJV)

The Bedroom

I awoke the next morning not understanding or giving much thought to fixing up God's house as He had told me to do the day before. I sat up in bed and saw before me a vision of an entire bedroom. It was as if I were standing in the doorway looking into someone else's room. I was overwhelmed at its beauty and amazed at the intricate detail on each piece of furniture.

First I noticed a dresser and a bureau. The faces of both pieces of furniture were bowed out and spacious, having many drawers. Both pieces of furniture were trimmed in ivory and gold and looked to be the color of birch wood.

The drawers opened with diamond handles, and ivory and gold feathers covered the upper corners of the mirror. The wood had distinct markings. The bureau also had ivory and gold feathers at each corner and drawers with handles of gold. It opened twice, to many compartments, with each drawer lined in a white silk.

The white walls to this room shimmered as they reflected the diamonds throughout the room. The windows were covered with white nylon curtains with a hint of maroon that could only be seen as the wind

Chapter 1

blew them back and forth. In the north-west corner was a rocking chair. It too seemed to have been made from the same wood as the bureau and dresser. It had a corduroy cream colored cushioned back and seat and a small plaid throw draped over the arm. The throw matched the comforter on the bed, and the pillow in the chair matched the pillows on the bed.

The throw and comforter were a deep, rich maroon and gray with a blue I had never seen before. It was a dusty, dark greyish blue. The blue separated the maroon and gray squares which gave an illusion of having no distinct lines to separate them. The cream colored fringes encircling the comforter complemented the rich colors and gave the room its masculine tone. The solid colored pillows matched the throw and comforter.

The bed had a canopy whose hangings draped over ivory and gold tusks. These hangings were made of nylon and matched the curtains at the window. They too had a hint of maroon that was made visible only by the wind. The headboard was made of pure diamond with gold woven throughout.

Over the closet was a valance of gold secured by ivory hooks. The closet door handles were two inches long and made of diamonds. The closet contained only wedding gowns secured on a rack similar to that at a dry cleaner that rotated at the push of a button. It was an endless rack of gowns of all sizes and shapes, each unique in design. Some glistened more than others, and some had diamonds underneath an outer nylon layer. The diamonds were all small but different shapes and sizes. Despite their sizes, however, the radiance from them was the closet's light.

In an instant the vision of that beautiful room was gone, and a vision of another room appeared before me. The condition of this bedroom was more outdated

Chapter 1

than my natural bedroom. The dresser and bureau were not at all like the ones I had just seen.

Most of the furniture was falling apart, and none of the furniture was in the same places as in the first vision. Not only was there no chair in the north-west corner of the room, but there was no chair at all. No throw, no gold valance with ivory hooks over the closet door and no diamond handles for opening the door. No canopy, no pillows or shiny handles anywhere. The curtains were close to what was in the first room, but they were not clean. The only thing close to the first room was the walls.

The Lord told me the first room was how He wanted His room within my heart to look. He said He desired it even more than I desired changes to my house, and this second dark, cold, unkempt room that was now before me was how it currently looked. He said that until things were in place He could not have the rest He sought. He then told me He wanted to show me what it would take to change it to how He wanted it to be.

I always thought I was the perfect wife. I always had food ready for my husband when he came home from work. I don't yell; I don't nag; I'm not bossy. So those things made me think my husband had a jewel in me but none of my attributes meant as much to the Lord as what was in my heart. The bible tells us that God looks on the heart. "But the Lord said unto Samuel, Look not on his countenance, or on the height of his stature because I have refused him: for the Lord seeth not as man seeth; for man looketh on the outward appearance, but the Lord looketh on the heart. (1 Sam 16:7 KJV) No matter how perfect I was in my own eyes, it was and is what's in my heart that matters most to God. What He showed me about myself humbled me.

Chapter 1

It's funny how God knows the deep things in our hearts—even from the smallest suppressed feeling of anger to the tiniest hint of deception. He requires truth in the inward parts: "Behold, thou desirest truth in the inward parts: and in the hidden part thou shalt make me to know wisdom" (Psalm 51:6, KJV). He requires it because this is where He resides. That's why He is constantly working in us tugging on our hearts, convicting us by His Spirit, as He creates within us a heart that is pure and true where He might find a place of rest.

I've always had a burden for marriages, so I've tried hard to be what I thought was a good wife by loving the Lord and allowing Him to guide me and help me understand how this not-so-easy union could work. I'm glad God knows us so much better than we know ourselves and can see what is even hidden from us.

Over the next few weeks the Lord took me through His entire house within my heart and showed me how to make the changes necessary for Him to abide and truly rest within His home in my heart.

CHAPTER 2

Remodelling the Bedroom

O Lord, thou hast searched me and known me. Thou knowest my downsitting and mine uprising, thou understandest my thought afar off. (Psalm 139:1)

The Bureau

First, we concentrated on the bureau. The bureau was square, plain and off-white. It had four drawers, and one of them was falling off its track. The Lord told me the condition of the bureau represented my anger or ill thoughts toward my husband.

It takes a lot for me to get mad, so I didn't understand why the condition of this bureau was so horrible. I was convinced the Lord had me mixed up with someone else. But then He told me my annoyances at my husband, which I kept to myself, were the silent kind of anger but were still anger. I even kept a smile on my face. Although I walked around annoyed on the inside and these feelings were hidden from those around me, they were not hidden from God. They were affecting the bureau in His bedroom. When we are annoyed or angry outwardly, especially as Christians, those around us can see our flaws. Some may even confront us, and this holds us accountable by making us aware of it. When we decide not to be annoyed that's good; but when we hold on to the annoyance and push it inward we can fool those around us and even ourselves, but we cannot fool God because his bureau becomes unsightly.

Chapter 2

As the psalmist writes,

O Lord, thou hast searched me and known me. Thou knowest my downsitting and mine uprising, thou understandest my thought afar off. Thou compassest my path and my lying down, and art acquainted with all my ways. For there is not a word in my tongue, but, lo, O Lord, thou knowest it altogether. Thou hast beset me behind and before, and laid thine hand upon me. Such knowledge is too wonderful for me; it is high, I cannot attain unto it. Whither shall I go from thy spirit? or whither shall I flee from thy presence? If I ascend up into heaven, thou art there: if I make my bed in hell, behold, thou art there. If I take the wings of the morning, and dwell in the uttermost parts of the sea; even there shall thy hand lead me, and thy right hand shall hold me. If I say, Surely the darkness shall cover me; even the night shall be light about me. Yea, the darkness hideth not from thee; but the night shineth as the day: the darkness and the light are both alike to thee. For thou hast possessed my reins: thou hast covered me in my mother's womb. I will praise thee; for I am fearfully and wonderfully made: marvellous are thy works; and that my soul knoweth right well. My substance was not hid from thee, when I was made in secret, and curiously wrought in the lowest parts of the earth. Thine eyes did see my substance, yet being unperfect; and in thy book all my members were written, which in continuance were fashioned, when as yet there was none of them. How precious also are thy thoughts unto me, O God! how great is the sum of them! If I should count them, they are more in number than the sand: when I awake, I am still with thee (Psalm 139:1-18, KJV).

After asking how to deal with this, two Scripture passages came to mind to pray: "Create in me a clean heart, O God; and renew a right spirit within me" (Psalm 51:10) and "Search me, O God, and know my heart: try me, and know my thoughts: and see if there be any wicked way in me, and lead me in the way everlasting" (Psalm 139:23-24).

Everyone gets annoyed, but whom we are annoyed with may affect our relationship with the Lord differently. Wives are told to reverence their husbands. In doing so, our thoughts should be nothing less than adoration. Our relationship with our husbands reflects our relationship with the Lord. When I would get angry with my husband and go into my prayer closet, I could feel the Lord literally turn His back to me. After asking for forgiveness and making things right with my husband, I'd entered the prayer closet and could sense the Lord standing there with open arms. No matter how much I didn't want to apologize at times and even if it wasn't my fault, I knew that if I wanted my relationship with the Lord to be right, things had to be good in my heart toward my husband.

In reverencing our husbands, we are to look up to them because they are our head and the head is above: "For the husband is the head of the wife, even as Christ is head of the church: and he is the savior of the body" (Ephesians 5:23).

When we have any thoughts other than those of adoration, these not-so-good thoughts takes us out of our place. Some feelings and thoughts put us on top, and we become the head looking down at them as a judge. When we are in place as judge we are on top

Chapter 2

looking down. When we don't like them we are definitely not looking up at them in reverence. With a pure and true heart toward our husbands we can remain in our God-appointed position and rest knowing that what God has for us He will give us and direct us. When we are out of position we are out of the will of God. When I say a pure and true heart it's just that. The Lord knows when we are genuine. He tells us in Matthew 18:35, "So likewise shall my heavenly father do also unto you if ye from your hearts forgive not everyone his brother their trespasses." How much more should this forgiveness apply to our spouses with whom we are joined as one. If we find this difficult to do we can ask Him for help and He will help us because it is the will of God that we forgive from our hearts.

When I first started working on the Lord's house my husband and I had a disagreement. I sat in bed attempting to read the Bible, and the Lord spoke to me and told me to apologize, even though I knew it wasn't my fault. Surely God knew it wasn't my fault. I couldn't believe He wanted me to apologize. But as an obedient servant I used all of my strength and went into the family room, said "I'm sorry" and walked away. I hadn't taken five steps before the Lord told me to mean it. I took a deep breath then turned around, yielded to the Lord for strength to do what I didn't really want to do but was willing. I looked my husband in the eyes with a now-softened heart and said, "Hey, honey, I'm sorry. Please forgive me." Saying those words from my heart gave me peace. Who was at fault no longer mattered. My husband forgave me.

The Lord then told me that since I was the Christian I needed to apologize because my husband didn't know its importance. He didn't have Christ living inside him nor was he, my husband, on a journey with the Lord; I was. We cannot even walk the true Christian walk

Chapter 2

in our own strength the way God wants us to; but we can if we allow the Lord to work in us and allow Him to make us not only into his dwelling place but into His resting place. If we can't be a Christian to our husbands or those in our households first, we are hypocrites. As a Christian it is easy to be nice or try to love our fellow Christians or strangers who do not live with us. But our true Christian walk is challenged and should be expressed first at home. How can we reach out to others and not to those in our own households? We often forget they are people too.

During the following weeks I tried not to get annoyed with my husband. I'm not talking about the anger you feel when your husband does something to make you mad; I didn't get mad at my husband too often like I said earlier, but I'm talking about the anger you feel when he doesn't do what you think he should, the way you think he should, or if he doesn't act or respond the way you want him to in certain situations. This is the annoyance I am speaking of. This was difficult at first. When I became a sold-out, born-again Christian a year after we got married I became "holy," and I didn't like the unholy advice my husband gave our children. Not because it wasn't okay advice but because I didn't agree with how he thought and he wasn't quoting the Bible to them. I would interfere and put my "holier than thou" two cents in to make sure they heard what they should.

Only God in His awesome power and in His sweet subtle way could have stripped this mindset from the deep core of my being without leaving any scars. That way of thinking was embedded in my skin. As I yielded to Him to help me, before I knew it I was at peace when I heard my husband talking to the kids. I either walked away or kept doing what I was doing, and it didn't bother me to do so.

Chapter 2

The Lord helped me realize my husband was his own person. He was not me. He had a mind of his own, thoughts of his own, opinions of his own, just as I did. And God created him to form him into the image of His Son Jesus Christ—not for me to mold him into the image of me.

I finally stopped getting angry when he remained cool and collected when I thought He should be angry, or when his advice to our children was not as "spiritual" as I thought it should be. "He is who he is, and he is not me," I told myself over and over again. This Scripture verse was then placed on my heart: *"Who art thou that judges another man's servant? To his own master he stands or falls"* (Romans 14:4). I rehearsed these living words constantly, and within no time at all they became a part of me. It's interesting how much these attitudes weigh us down without our realizing it, until they are lifted away.

To digress, I do not want to make it sound as if we must accept everything our husbands say and do, nor are the husbands to accept what the wife says and does if it is truly something to be concerned with. I wanted my husband to speak my words only and think my thoughts only, especially when it came to our children.

I began accepting his way of thinking as his way, and, I assure you, only God could have helped me with this. For fifty or so years I believed everyone thought the way I did. I thought I had the only good advice and that only my answers to problems were correct. I never knew this was a problem, but I'm glad God knew about it and its detriment, and only He and His word could have dug deep into my thoughts and put the correct thinking there. "For the word of God is quick, and powerful, and sharper than any two-edged sword, piercing even to the dividing asunder of soul and spirit, and of the joints and marrow, and

Chapter 2

is a discerner of the thoughts and intents of the heart" (Hebrews 4:12, KJV).

I wish I could tell you how big of an issue this was. You know the saying "you can't teach an old dog new tricks." Well, that sums it up, but with God all things are possible.

Soon these living words became part of me, and more and more I felt as if weights were being removed from my shoulders.

Now when my husband is talking to our kids I listen sometimes if I'm close, not intentionally but with total peace. And I am reminded each time of the miracle the Lord did in me, simply by yielding to him and I smile. Even if I did not agree with my husband all the time, who cared? I understood and accepted that his way of thinking was simply not my way, and it wasn't a bad way of thinking; nor was his advice detrimental. The biggest revelation to have was to realize that my children were in God's hands and His hands are bigger than mine.

Eventually this helped to transform the Lord's bureau into the one He desired, and it began to remove a heaviness from me that I wasn't aware of. A precious calm came over me each time I refused to become angry and chose to accept my husband and his way of thinking. I realized that being a Christian I am not here to change others but to draw them to Christ by how I live my own life. As I began truly dealing with this problem it felt as if links to a chain wrapped around me had began to be removed one link at a time. How awesome God can be if only we will yield to His Spirit for help.

A few weeks after this issue was dealt with a challenging situation arose that finally took away any struggle that remained. I got annoyed with my husband for not responding to a situation the way I thought he

Chapter 2

should, and as I mentioned before I never voiced my disappointments in my husband to my husband. He never knew I struggled with this crippling issue.

Don't think I don't voice my opinion from time to time. I'm not trying to paint a perfect picture of myself, but I kept a lot of anger inside that only the Lord knew about.

On this particular day the Lord revealed that the condition of His bureau had returned to its original state. I then felt the Lords pain as he desperately waited for the condition of my heart to be right so that he can truly rest within me. I felt as if I were Judas who had betrayed the Lord or Peter who denied Him. This pain, however, gave me a new determination and strength to yield one hundred percent to Him and allow Him to do whatever it took to create His resting place in my heart.

I would like to say that after struggling with my flesh and tromping through muddy terrain, and with many nights of fasting, praying, and sitting in sackcloth and ashes, I accomplished this task. But in only a few weeks with the revelation of this heavenly bureau I simply yielded, and the Lord did it all. He removed my old way of thinking and replaced it with the correct way of thinking. Even my heart begin to soften more and more towards my husband. Who knew?

The Dresser

...cursed is the ground for thy sake; in sorrow shalt thou eat of it all the days of thy life; Thorns also and thistles shall it bring forth to thee; and thou shalt eat the herb of the field; In the sweat of thy face shalt thou eat bread, till thou return unto the ground for out of it wast thou taken: for dust thou art and unto dust shalt thou return. (Genesis 3:17-18

Chapter 2

Next we worked on the dresser. What an embarrassing state this dresser was in. Unlike the one the Lord wanted, it was painted dark brown. The paint was so chipped that it was hard at first to tell where the paint ended and the actual dresser begin. My dresser was taller than the bureau and looked oversized and out of place.

Although the dresser goes hand-in-hand with the bureau, it represents our attitudes when our husbands get on our nerves. It is that disgusted-with-them attitude we get when they do not act like the heroic knights in shining armour they once were to us, and we wish they were like so and so. Or when they are simply wrong and we are right; when we see their human side along with their frailties and insecurities; when we see little boys instead of men; even when they treat us as if we are children. The Lord told me any unpleasant thoughts or feelings I had toward my husband would cause the dresser to become unsightly to Him.

I realized that even though I had pushed those feelings aside with a "whatever" attitude the feelings did not go away. Instead they went straight to the Lord's house in my heart to become His dresser. The strange thing about the dresser the Lord wanted was that the frame for the mirror had ivory and gold feathers at each corner but no mirror. When I asked the Lord why, He told me the mirror would be added only when He could look in it and not see us. Such as our pride or our wrong attitudes, but could see His own reflection.

To destroy them we must choose not to feel them. Sure, no problem, right?

As the Lord helped me to understand the enormous responsibility placed on a man's shoulders when he has a wife and family, it became easier to control my attitude. I could actually feel his burden. He said the

Chapter 2

burden is there whether or not the man is responsible, whether or not he knows how to be a good steward of money, whether or not he knows how to love his wife or his children. In many cases, its weight is why men run.

Unto Adam he said, Because thou has harkened unto the voice of thy wife, and has eaten of the tree of which I commanded thee, saying Thou shalt not eat of it: cursed is the ground for thy sake; in sorrow shalt thou eat of it all the days of thy life; Thorns also and thistles shall it bring forth to thee; and thou shalt eat the herb of the field; In the sweat of thy face shalt thou eat bread, till thou return unto the ground for out of it wast thou taken: for dust thou art and unto dust shalt thou return. (Genesis 3:17-18

This is why sometimes husbands look at their wives and wonder why they don't understand. No one realizes that it is this burden we do not understand.

. . . and they two shall become one

Suddenly I sensed his fears, worry and pain in not just wanting to provide for his wife and children but needing to do so. The responsibility can be overwhelming, and sometimes they are frustrated because they don't understand a burden they were never meant to bear alone.

Once I shared with the Lord how frustrated I was about my husband not doing what I thought he should be doing to be the example I thought he should be. He told me to concentrate on fixing His house in my heart; it was my responsibility alone to create the house He wanted in my heart, and only my husband could create the house God wanted in his heart. If he did, he did; and if he didn't, it was not my responsibility to make him create a house for the Lord to abide in. It was his choice to allow Christ to create a place for Him to abide in, and I should be concerned with showing my husband Christ instead of trying to make him fulfill

Chapter 2

my purpose for him. It is however the Lords desire that everyone will be saved. "The Lord is not slack concerning his promise, as some men count slackness; but is longsuffering to us-ward, not willing that any should perish, but that all should come to repentance." (II Peter 3:9)

Concentrating on decorating the Lord's house began to excite me and put hope in my heart. Once I mastered my attitude the dresser seemed more beautiful than when the Lord first showed it to me. With both pieces of furniture intact, God's peace filled me more and more. Two pieces of furniture complete with an entire house to go!

We spent more time fixing up the bedroom than any other room in His house. He told me the bedroom was the most important room. He said it was not a coincidence it had the most intricate and detailed furnishings. It takes time to build these pieces, just as it takes time to perfect them in our hearts. It is in the bedroom, He said, that the whole house rests. When this room is in place it is easier to put the rest of the house in place. Here relationships with our husbands are truly expressed, as is our relationship with the Lord expressed in His bedroom within our hearts.

If our hearts and thoughts are pure toward our husbands they are pure before the Lord. The only difference is that our husbands can't see our hearts, but God can. Our relationships with our husbands reflect our relationship with the Lord.

The Walls

> *... and she despised him in her heart (2 Samuel 6:16)*

The walls of my bedroom were already as He desired. But He told me that when we despise our

Chapter 2

husbands the walls become spotted and full of mold from the inside out. He explained that despising our husbands will cause them to be deceived as well as prevent us from producing real spiritual fruit. We become spiritually barren. David's wife Michal despised him and was barren until her death . II Samuel 6:16-23 reads,

"And as the ark of the Lord came into the city of David, Michal Saul's daughter looked through a window, and saw king David leaping and dancing before the Lord; and she despised him in her heart.

And they brought in the ark of the Lord, and set it in his place, in the midst of the tabernacle that David had pitched for it: and David offered burnt offerings and peace offerings before the Lord.

And as soon as David had made an end of offering burnt offerings and peace offerings, he blessed the people in the name of the Lord of host.

. . . and they two shall become one

And he dealt among all the people, even among the whole multitude of Israel, as well to the women as men, to every one a cake of bread, and a good piece *of flesh*, and a flagon *of wine*. So all the people departed everyone to his house.

Then David returned to bless his household. And Michal the daughter of Saul came out to meet David, and said, How glorious was the king of Israel to day, who uncovered himself to day in the eyes of the handmaids of his servants, as one of the vain fellows shamelessly uncovereth himself!

And David said unto Michal, It was before the Lord, which chose me before my father, and before all his house, to appoint me ruler over the people of the Lord, over Israel: therefore will I play before the Lord.

And I will yet be more vile than thus, and will be base in mine own sight: and of the maidservants which thou hast spoken of, of them shall I be had in honour.

Chapter 2

Therefore Michal the daughter of Saul had no child unto the day of her death."

Now my attitudes representing the bureau and the dresser are different from that of the walls. With one piece I wanted him to think like I wanted him to and with the other I wanted him to act like I wanted him to act. To despise is different. According to Webster's II New Riverside University Dictionary, Despise means 1. To regard with scorn or contempt 2. To regard with extreme hostility or dislike 3. To regard as trivial or worthless. Its easy for a homeowner to be deceived into thinking the house is intact by looking at the outside, unaware that the walls inside are rotting because of the mold within the walls. In the same way our husbands are deceived when they think things are intact; they don't realize their walls to their marital foundation are moldy from the wife despising the husband.

I tried to think pleasant thoughts toward my husband whenever I got upset with him. I feared my anger or annoyances turning into my despising him. I prayed good things for him and thanked the Lord for the good things about him: The following scripture is so powerful and helped give me the strength to keep pleasant thoughts about him ever present. "Finally, brethren, whatsoever things are true, whatsoever things are honest, whatsoever things are just, whatsoever things are pure, whatsoever things are lovely, whatsoever things are of good report; if there be any virtue, and if there be any praise, think on these things" (Philippians 4:7-8). Even if there's only one good thing. Think on that one good thing. Make sure it is instead of the bad thing or things.

The Bed and the Closet

"Defraud ye not one the other except it be with consent for a time, that ye may give

Chapter 2

yourselves to fasting and prayer; and come together again that Satan tempt you not for your incontinency" (1 Corinthians 7:5, KJV).

Next we worked on the bed and closet. Oddly, though, they represented the same thing. The bed was made but not as He wanted it. The comforter He wanted for the bed was different from the one I had. The comforter He wanted was beautiful with large tassels at each corner. The strings of the tassels were a quarter inch thick and made of gold. Part of the comforter hung over each tassel. The comforter, like the curtains, shimmered occasionally and was interwoven with diamond threads.

One large pillow with tassels on each end stretched across the entire width of the headboard. Other pillows looked like feathers with gold down the center of them.

There was only one wedding gown in the closet. He told me this represents intimacy with my husband. When we deny our husbands intercourse our bed isn't made, the covers are torn and dirty and the wedding gown has no diamonds on it, and black spots form in their place. Our agreement with our husbands puts the diamonds on the gown. Although He had numerous gowns in His closet representing many believers, there was only the one gown in His personal closet in my heart which represented me.

Scripture tells us as married couples not to deny one another sex unless it is with mutual consent for prayer and fasting. "Defraud ye not one the other except it be with consent for a time, that ye may give yourselves to fasting and prayer; and come together again that Satan tempt you not for your incontinency" (1 Corinthians 7:5, KJV). Notice this applies to the marriage relationship. As wives, the bible also tells us

Chapter 2

that we do not have power or control over our bodies but our husbands do. Neither does the husband has power or control over his own body but the wife. "The wife hath not power of her own body, but the husband: and likewise also the husband hath not power of his own body, but the wife" (1 Corinthians 7:4, KJV). This is not intended to abuse one another but when we give ourselves in marriage there is a mutual understanding to love, honour and cherish one another.

Notice that the verse before this says to come together quickly after fasting and prayer so that we won't be tempted for our incontinency or weakness. This is a problem many men face. Their wives deny them sex and use it as a tool. If you are a woman or a man and do this you shouldn't. We should communicate and work things out instead.

The Bible does not say to have sex only when you are one hundred percent happy with your spouse. The bible also tells the husbands to love the wife as Christ loves the church. "Husbands, love your wives, even as Christ also loved the church, and gave himself for it. (Ephesians 5:25 KJV) If you do not feel like it, pray and yield to the Holy Spirit, and you may soon be in the mood. When Jesus was faced with the cross before Him, He yielded and was ministered to and strengthen to go on. "Saying, Father if thou be willing, remove this cup from me: nevertheless not my will, but thine, be done. And there appeared an angel unto him from heaven strengthening him" (Luke 22:42-43). We have access to this same strength. If Jesus yielded and got to the cross we can have sex with one another even when conditions are not perfect if the other has the desire at least try if at all possible to fulfill it

A personal note: Many times I have taken on a burden from someone and will pray for them until the burden lifts. One day as I was praying for a young

Chapter 2

man who had a horrible struggle with lust, the Lord allowed me to feel what he felt. Lust is the most powerful spirit I've ever faced, and I have faced many. It took three weeks to get rid of this spirit. No other spirit I have dealt with ever took that long. No matter where I was or what I was doing I could only think of sex. I had no desire for any man other than my husband, but I wanted sex with him all the time. Lust was on my mind all the time so I prayed continuously. After three weeks the burden lifted. The heaviness was gone. Lust is very powerful. This is something to be mindful of whenever our spouse desires to be intimate.

From the work in the bedroom alone, I realized how much our feelings toward our husbands can affect not only our walk with the Lord, but also their walk with the Lord. As I yielded to the Lord, His bedroom finally came together, and I felt refreshed inside and out. I could sense Christ within me more as each piece of furniture was complete.

The Curtains and the Chair

Wives submit yourselves unto your *own* husbands as unto the Lord. (Ephesians 5:22)

The beauty of the curtains is maintained when we keep personal, intimate, marital business to ourselves. When we talk about the things that should only be shared with our husbands or kept between the two of you we take away from the beauty of the curtains. God says these things should be private. He gave me Ephesians 5:22 which says, "Wives submit yourselves unto your *own* husbands as unto the Lord." At first I thought this meant I am not to submit to another woman's husband. But as I studied the word "own" in the Strong's Exhaustive

Chapter 2

Concordance #2398 in the Greek it means – pertaining to self, i.e. One's own. Private or separate: his acquaintance, when they were alone, apart.

The chair in the North-West corner of the bedroom represents peace within the entire house. This chair would not be there unless all things in the house are as the Lord desires. This, He said, is where the He rests and blesses the relationship in a way not many experience.

CHAPTER 3

The Dining Room

"Speak not evil one of another, brethren. He that speaks evil of his brother and judges his brother speaks evil of the law and judges the law. But if you judge the law you are not a doer of the law, but a judge" (James 4:11, KJV).

The dining room I had in my heart was very interesting. Only a table stood there with chairs around it. It was the dining room in my actual home. It was not in bad shape, just outdated. A light from above shone on it.

Chapter 3

The dining room the Lord wanted was very different. I had never seen more beautiful pieces of furniture. The chairs alone took my breath away and brought tears to my eyes. Each chair had fabric in the seat and on the back. The fabric was white with a silver hue. Fabric was also between the wood on the arms of the two end chairs. The table was elegant. The top of the table was designed to look like a tablecloth draped over the sides. The light above the table was too bright to look at but gave off just the right amount of light from a distance. God explained to me that this room represented how we speak to our husbands in public. If we speak well of them in public the furniture is as God wants it; if we do not, the furniture will not be as He wants.

This light, He told me is the light of judgment. It shines brightly on what we say about our husbands in public. "Speak not evil one of another, brethren. He that speaks evil of his brother and judges his brother speaks evil of the law and judges the law. But if you judge the law you are not a doer of the law, but a judge" (James 4:11, KJV). A judge sits higher than others. We take this place when we speak evil of our husbands. We become their judge looking down on them thus stepping out of our place which is underneath them looking up to them. Jesus reminds us, "Judge not and you shall not be judged" (Luke 6:37, KJV). When we become the judge looking down we are out of place and cannot receive the flow of blessings that comes through our heads, our husbands. When we speak well of them we are looking up at them, adoring them. Ephesians 5:23 says, "For the husband is the head of the wife, even as Christ is the head of the church." And 1 Corinthians 11:3 says, "But I would have you know, that the head of every man is Christ, and the head of the woman is the man, and the head of Christ is God."

Chapter 3

The head is on top. Even though we are equal and one in God's eyes and are all the body of Christ, there is an ordained order.

The Kitchen

"Behold, thou desirest truth in the inward parts.." (Psalm 51:6a, KJV).

A table in the kitchen represented our times of informal dining and revealed the condition of our family relationships. The refrigerator represented what we feed our husbands and family. When we talk negative to them or speak discouraging words to them the food in His refrigerator becomes mouldy and the milk is spoiled. If we talk positive and use encouraging words the food remains fresh, and the refrigerator smells clean.

The kitchen had no cabinets, just drawers. Each drawer was filled with only knives. The knives represented the times we stab our husbands in the back. This occurs when we withhold information from them or go against what they say. I began to see a knife in my husband's back one day in a vision and knew exactly why it was there. It was a result of my making a purchase on our credit against his wishes. I knew he did not want me to do it, but I thought I would be able to pay it off without him knowing about it. The Lord requires truth in the inward parts. "Behold, thou desirest truth in the inward parts.." (Psalm 51:6a, KJV). Even if no one knows if we are honest or not He does. We are blessed to have our hearts always before the Lord.

The Family Room

…. and they took knowledge of them, that they had been with Jesus." (Acts 4:13b, KJV).

Chapter 3

The family room in the Lord's house is the place where we commune with Him. The condition of this room represents our relationship with Him. This is where He examines our hearts as we sit quietly before Him, taking in His presence, allowing ourselves to draw from Him as He imparts to us His fruit of the Spirit. It's where He knows us and where fruit is birthed. Adam "knew" Eve in Genesis 4:1, and she conceived and bore a son. So it is with us. As we "know" Him intimately, we will bear His fruit. As we allow ourselves to reside in this place it should become aware to those around us, even at home, that we have been with Him just as it was with Peter and John.

"Now when they saw the boldness of Peter and John, and perceived that they were unlearned and ignorant men, they marvelled; and they took knowledge of them, that they had been with Jesus." (Acts 4:13, KJV).

The Bathroom

So likewise shall my heavenly Father do also unto you, if ye from your hearts forgive not every one his brother their trespasses (Mathew 18:35)

I thought the Lord's house was finished until He woke me in the night and told me we still had to talk about the bathroom. I laughed at the thought of the Lord talking about the bathroom. Only a toilet was present in the bathroom. The toilet represented our ability to forgive. If we do not forgive one another the toilet remains full of waste. When we forgive from our hearts. He flushes all the waste away never to be seen again.

So likewise shall my heavenly Father do also unto you, if ye from your hearts forgive not every one his brother their trespasses (Mathew 18:35)

Chapter 3

The Attic and the Basement

Being confident of this very thing, that he which hath begun a good work in you will perform it until the day of Jesus Christ. (Philippians 1:6)

The attic and the basement are the places where He stores visions not yet fulfilled while we wait on Him to bring to pass what He has placed in our spirits. Even though they are stored, they are not inaccessible. From time to time as we sit alone with him he pulls them to the forefront of our minds to keep them ever alive until he accomplishes in us his purpose and will.

Being confident of this very thing, that he which hath begun a good work in you will perform it until the day of Jesus Christ. (Philippians 1:6)

The Garden

Come unto me, all ye that labour and are heavy laden, and I will give you rest. Take my yoke upon you, and learn of me; for I am meek and lowly in heart: and ye shall find rest unto your souls. (Matthew 11:28)

Some needs even a spouse cannot meet, and even the best marriage cannot bring the peace that can only come from Jesus Christ. Whatever our husbands Cannot be, whatever the wife cannot be, God can be. He is truly all and all.

The Lord spoke these words to me: *"Let not thy heart be troubled over things of this world. Has your love denied thee of My precious fruits? Care not for things that pertain unto this world. Neither let thy concerns trouble thee. Smell in My garden the lilies and fresh fruits of Spain, the chrysanthemums and roses*

Chapter 3

of great delight. Come out to My garden and walk among the flowers. Sit beside the waters and receive refreshing. Let Me be thy desire. Let only lack of My company become a burden because My company is needed. I know all things, but do you realize who has control over thee? Let it be Me and let it not be concerns of what thou cannot change. Cease from strife. Strive for peace. Be in unity. Be ONE so that I can work on thy behalf. Worry not about where thy love may take thee, but I say to thee, come out into My garden and receive from me thy refreshing."

A garden lies outside His home within our hearts. Our hearts search for that place of rest. In spending quiet times in His presence, allowing His Spirit to refresh and renew our spirits, we find the rest necessary to allow His Spirit to roam freely throughout His house within our hearts.

. . . and they two shall become one

Come unto me, all ye that labour and are heavy laden, and I will give you rest. Take my yoke upon you, and learn of me; for I am meek and lowly in heart and ye shall find rest unto your souls. (Matthew 11:28)

CHAPTER 4

The Jewel of Submission

Wives, submit yourselves unto your own husbands, as unto the Lord (Ephesians 5:22)

*S*ubmission sets the tone for the atmosphere in the home. I had been saved for only three months and had been attending a new church for about a month. My husband started getting angry each time I came home. We began to argue about that church. Each time I wanted to tell him I wouldn't attend anymore I started to cry. I was so in love with the Lord, and all I wanted was to feel His presence and hear His Word being preached.

One day after arguing with my husband about the church I stood at the window in tears and asked the Lord what I should do. He spoke softly to me and told me to submit. I instantly went to my husband and told him I would not attend that church anymore, and I had peace inside. I knew the Lord was directing me because the thought of not going didn't bother me this time. This happened on a Thursday.

On Saturday, two days later, my husband came to me and asked me if I was going to church the next day. I told him I didn't have a church to go to and had to find another one. He reached out to me and told me he knew I enjoyed the church we often argued about, but he gave me his blessing to go there. So I did, and we never had another issue about that church again.

Chapter 4

On another occasion my aunt died. After making arrangements with my mom and brother to go to the funeral I spoke to my husband about our plans; I felt sure within myself that I was expected to go. I had three young daughters at the time who were not in school, so I thought it would work out fine. Instead my husband told me he didn't want me to go. It was very unlike him and unusual for someone to say they didn't want you going to a funeral. I didn't understand. After he saw how determined I was to go he told me he would take off work to watch the girls while I went, but I was not taking the girls with me.

It didn't make sense to me. Who doesn't go to funerals? After seeking the Lord's advice I felt that I was once again to submit, so I did. I told my mom and my brother that I couldn't go. I wasn't happy about what was going on, but I stayed behind.

My mom and my brother left Detroit on a Friday morning heading for the funeral in Little Rock, Arkansas. The next day I received a call from my mom telling me that it was a good thing I didn't come or bring the girls. The authorities closed down all roads in Kentucky due to an ice storm, and my mom and my brother ended up spending three nights sleeping in a mall. My mom said it was very cold and was the most uncomfortable experience she'd ever had. I realized it was the Lord directing me through my husband. From that time on, I listened to my husband in everything and knew the Lord would work through him if I submitted. This doesn't mean I didn't voice my opinion but if it turned into an argument and when I saw that I wasn't getting through to my husband I quickly submitted to him.

Even when it came to choosing the children's school God used my husband to direct them. One day

Chapter 4

I was praying for my oldest daughter. I was seeking the Lord as to what school He wanted her to attend. I had already signed her up for the local public middle school, but I kept everything in prayer until I knew things were in place as the Lord wanted. One morning as I prayed I kept hearing the name of a school in my mind. The next day I saw some friends of mine, and the Lord spoke to me and said He wanted my daughter to go to the same school my friends' daughter attended. It was a private school and was the name of the school I had heard Him speak to me while in prayer. I had not heard of this school before. I told my husband excitedly when he got home about how the Lord confirmed where He wanted my daughter to go. My husband became very upset and said, "No! we are not going to shelter our kids."

I told him it wasn't sheltering and that I believed that was where she was supposed to go. He didn't budge. I told him the devil would love me to argue, but I wouldn't. If it was the Lord, and I knew it was, it would work out. I then submitted to him by saying okay. I went on with the plans to have my daughter go to the local middle school. I signed her up to play the drums in the band and continued to get her connected and registered there.

Two days later my husband called me from work and asked if we still had time to sign our daughter up at the private school. It was the last day of registration. I told him it wasn't too late. He then gave me the green light and said sign her up. He ended up telling me to enroll all three of our daughters, and I did.

A similar thing happened concerning the children's schools. After being at that private school for five years I sensed the Lord telling me to visit a particular church for two Sundays in a row. I went the first Sunday and couldn't see why He wanted me to

Chapter 4

go but went back the next Sunday. During that service I looked on the back of the bulletin and realized they had a school.

It's funny how the Lord knew it would take me those two Sundays before I turned the bulletin over. I felt that the Lord wanted me to have the girls change schools. I have been feeling it for a while but it wasn't until being here at this church that it was confirmed. After I prayed about it and was convinced this was where God was leading us I told my husband what I thought we should do.

Once again he blew up. He was even louder and angrier than the first private school deal. His anger wasn't attributed to the fact that he thought I had once again lost my mind but because the cost of the tuition at this new school was double the price of their current one. You do remember how long we had our furniture, right? Then you could imagine how unbudging my husband could be and was about this. "We are not going to pay more money for them to be sheltered at another one of these private schools!" he shouted. I simply said I felt the Lord wanted us to change schools. He then shouted, "then tell the Lord to pay for it." The case was closed and I didn't try to reopen it. I submitted and said that's okay. I kissed him and thought how the devil would love for me to argue; but I knew that if it was the Lord it would work out.

I went about my business, and a few days later my husband called me from work and asked if we still had time to enrol the girls at that other private school. I told him it was the last day, which it was, and he said why don't you go and sign them up; so I did.

It isn't necessarily private schools the Lord wants our children to attend. We want them wherever He wants them. The public school would have been okay with me if that was where God wanted them. I believe

Chapter 4

this lesson was so He could perfect in me the joy of submission. I can tell you about countless occasions when God worked through my husband as I submitted.

If you think I don't have a voice in my home you are correct. I am a woman whose silent submission speaks louder than arguing words ever could. My submission keeps the Lord flowing in my life

It wasn't always this way. I once called my husband "the king of controllers," and I was no doubt the "queen of you are not going to tell me what to do." He and I had our days of bumping heads, but the Lord is so good. He graciously showed me that submitting allows him to work on my behalf and He hasn't failed me yet. There have been times when I thought the Lord wanted me to do something and I submitted to my husband and it didn't happen. I thank the Lord for shutting that door for me and am convinced it didn't happened because the Lord truly did not in fact want me to do it. We are told however to submit one to another according to Ephesians 5:21 "Submitting yourselves one to another in the fear of God." The man is still placed in authority over the woman to rule or govern over her. Genesis 3:16 "Unto the woman he said, I will greatly multiply thy sorrow and thy conception; in sorrow thou shalt bring forth children; and thy desire shall be to thy husband, and he shall rule over thee." Within a year of my understanding of submission my controlling husband began submitting to me by listening to my opinion on things instead of being the only voice. The apostle Paul writes, "Wives, submit yourselves unto your own husbands, as it is fit in the Lord" (Colossians 3:18). He doesn't tell us to submit only if they act like we want them to. He simply says submit—as it is fit in the Lord. We are not to pick certain times when we want to submit and other times when we don't. If it isn't breaking the law its okay to submit instead of arguing. It is for us that we are told to do so.

When we pray or prophesy unsubmitted to our husbands we dishonor them because they are considered our head. "But every woman that prayeth or prophesieth with her head uncovered dishonoreth her head" (1 Corinthians 11:5, KJV). Verse 3 says, "But I would have you know, that the head of every man is Christ; and the head of the woman is the man; and the head of Christ is God." God has placed the man to govern his wife as the wife is to be in subjection to him.

CHAPTER 5

What about My Husband?

"Husbands, love your wives, even as Christ also loves the church and gave himself for it" (Ephesians 5:25).

For the past seven years I have been trying to keep the Lord's house in order. Just as I think I have accomplished it, I fall short and am reminded of the area in which I failed. God is faithful and will help us when we fall. All He wants is a willing heart and a yielded spirit.

Chapter 5

I asked the Lord why the wife had to do all the work and what role the husband played in all this. He in turn asked me, "Do you want to see the house your husband covers you with?" I answered, "Yes." And the home He showed me was so beautiful it could only be imagined in a dream. I asked the Lord to explain. He told me the condition of the inside of the house was my responsibility and the condition of the outside of the house was the husband's responsibility. When the two do their parts they create a complete home for Him. They two shall become one.

He continued to explain that the outside of the house is the "covering" and the beautiful house I saw was the actual covering my husband has over me. The house becomes beautiful and solid when the husband loves his wife as Christ loves the church: "Husbands, love your wives, even as Christ also loves the church and gave himself for it" (Ephesians 5:25). This word "love" according to *Strong's Exhaustive Concordance* of the bible means to focus. It is as if one has binoculars and zooms in on something—the something for the husband's focus is the wife. He is to pay close attention to her, making sure her needs are met and keeping constant watch that she is never sad; if she is sad he should find out why and do what he can to try to fix the problem.

He told me my husband meets all of my human needs (not my wants). When I am sad he notices, sits me down and tries to fix whatever is wrong. He said that is why my covering is so beautiful and solid. He showed me what happens when the husband does not love his wife as Christ loves the church.

The Roof

"Husbands, love your wives and be not bitter against them" (Colossians 3:19).

Chapter 5

The roof represents the husband's relationship with God. His relationship with his wife will mirror his relationship with God. When a man talks badly or thinks badly about his wife, holes appear in the roof; if he is bitter toward her the roof is removed. Rain can then get into the house and mess things up. This will happen even if he is angry with his wife. "Husbands, love your wives and be not bitter against them" (Colossians 3:19).

When the husband does not love his wife and is not concerned if she is happy or sad, the locks fall off the doors and windows because her needs are not met. The thief, our enemy the devil, comes in and steals. The thief will continue to come in and remove each brick, for each unmet need, until the frame becomes weak and eventually collapses.

This is the enemy's goal because he does not want the couple to stand on a solid foundation nor does he want a marriage to work. He knows the home is the foundation of families and that these two people can touch and agree at any time and whatever they ask for shall be done. "Again I say unto you, that if two of you shall agree on earth as touching anything that they shall ask, it shall be done for them of my Father which is in heaven" (Matthew 18:19). He (the enemy) knows that if these two agree to allow the Lord to build His house within their hearts, the Lord's city will be built one house at a time.

The commandment for the husbands to love their wives has no stipulations. Although the woman should make it easy for the man to love her the bible doesn't say to love her only when she is pleasant. In Proverbs 25:24, Solomon writes, "It is better to dwell in the corner of the housetop, than with a brawling woman in a wide house." The Lord said that when husbands look at other women a shovel is placed at the foundation of the house. When they lust after another woman in their hearts the shovel begins lifting the house off its foundation. causing it to lean and the entire household walks on that lean, and things in the house become distorted or off kilter. This is what Jesus said as he addressed the issue of adultery. He says, "But I say unto you, that whosoever looketh on a woman to lust after her hath committed adultery with her already in his heart" (Matthew 5:28, KJV)

I inquired further concerning the husband's role as I'm sure many women reading this book will also want to know. This is the Scripture verse the Lord gave me: "Peter seeing him saith to Jesus, Lord, and what shall this man do? Jesus saith unto him, if I will that he tarry till I come, what is that to thee? Follow thou me" (John 21:22, KJV).

The Floor

.... And they twain shall be one flesh (Matthew 19:5)

In Matthew 19:5 Jesus says, "For this cause shall a man leave father and mother, and shall cleave to his wife: and they twain shall be one flesh." This word "flesh" according to Strong's Exhaustive Concordance #4561 comes from the Greek word pronounced "sarx" which is from the base of #4563 which is "sar-o'-o" which means "to brush off—meaning a broom—or to sweep." When both husband and wife unite with the sole purpose of creating a place of rest for the Lord, the powerful broom of unity causes the floors to be swept thus creating the footstool for the Lord, making it holy Ground.

Chapter 5

Our Children

Martha, Martha, thou are careful and troubled about many things: but one thing is needful. (Luke 10:41b)

This is the only thing He said to me concerning our children. He said that disobedient children represent dust throughout the house. They cause the house to become dusty. We become busy like a "Martha" trying to dust and clean all the time. "And she had a sister called Mary, which also sat at Jesus' feet, and heard his word. But Martha was cumbered about much serving, and came to him and said, Lord, dost thou not care that my sister hath left me to serve alone? Bid her therefore that she help me. And Jesus answered and said unto her, Martha, Martha, thou are careful and troubled about many things: But one thing is needful:

and Mary hath chosen the good part, which shall not be taken away" (Luke 10:39-42)

The Air

Proverbs 20:27 "The spirit of man is the candle of the Lord, searching all the inward parts of the belly."

I was surprised that the Lord had me add even the air in the house to this collection of revelations but I wasn't surprised when he told me that trust is the air in the home. Even though trust is the key ingredient in any relationship for the man and for the woman. what was ironic to me and yet comforting was that He said it was the trust that the husband has in the wife that set this tone for His air. The reason why this was comforting and an easy concept to grasp was because I have always noticed that the wife of any pastor has always governed the atmosphere in the church by her disposition. Up until now I never knew why that was made clear to me, but now I see that it was a revelation from God. I have been to several churches during my almost twenty-two years as a Christian and one thing my spirit picks up on immediately as I enter the doors was that each church has a certain "air" about it and that air is always, always run or should I say governed by the disposition of the wife of that pastor.

Lets look at the very first wife Eve and see how she handled her position. It wasn't until after God gave Adam the command not to eat of the tree of the knowledge of good and evil that Eve was created.

Gen 2:16 "And the Lord God commanded the man, saying, Of every tree of the garden thou mayest freely eat:

. . . and they two shall become one

But of the tree of the knowledge of good and evil, thou shalt not eat of it: for in the day that thou eatest thereof thou shalt surely die.

And the Lord God said, it is not good that the man should be alone; I will make him an help meet for him,

And out of the ground the Lord God formed every beast of the field, and every fowl of the air; and brought them unto Adam to see what he would call them: and whatsoever Adam called every living creature, that was the name thereof

And Adam gave names to all cattle, and to the fowl of the air, and to every beast of the field; but for Adam there was not found an help meet for him.

and the Lord God caused a deep sleep to fall upon Adam, and he slept: and he took one of his ribs. And closed up the flesh instead thereof;

and the rib which the Lord God had taken from man, made he a woman and brought her unto the man"

Chapter 5

One thing Adam did do was warn Eve about the tree, otherwise, how would she have known when she was tempted by the Serpent. Let's take a look.

Genesis 3:1-2 reads, *Now the serpent was more subtle than any beast of the field which the Lord God had made. And he said unto the woman, yea, hath God said, ye shall not eat of every tree of the garden? And the woman said unto the serpent. We may eat of the fruit of the tree of the garden: But of the fruit of the tree which is in the midst of the garden, God hath said, Ye shall not eat of it, neither shall ye touch it, least ye die.*

It is clearly understood that the role of the woman has always been that of taking care of the house, caring for the children and preparing the meals for her family, etc. Typically the man works all day and comes home to a meal prepared by the wife. I know that this isn't the case for every household but in general, especially when

Eve was around, this was the custom. With this in mind Eve was entrusted with this task while in the garden. She was trusted to provide a meal for Adam. Should Adam have wondered what it was that they were eating? Should he have wondered if Eve could be trusted? He should have trusted that what she was feeding him was safe. There is a discrepancy about whether or not Adam knowingly took of the forbidden fruit, however, the bible clearly says that Adam was with Eve when she ate of it. "She took of the fruit thereof, and did eat, and gave also unto her husband with her; and he did eat." Genesis 3:6b. However, Eve was still the one who offered it to Adam and being with her does it simply mean the one who was in the garden with her?

Proverbs 31:10- 12 asks who can find a virtuous woman? It continues and says that her price is far above rubies. It tells us that the heart of her husband doth safely trust in her, so that he shall have no need

Chapter 5

of spoil. This virtuous woman will do him good and not evil all the days of her life.

> *""who can find a virtuous woman?" For her price is far above rubies. The heart of her husband safely trust in her; so that he shall have no need of spoil. She will do him good and not evil all the days of her life." (Proverbs 31:10-12)*

Proverbs 31:23 says that this virtuous woman's husband is also know in the gates. "Her husband is known in the gates, when he sitteth among the elders of the land." Not only was Eve not trust worthy with dinner she fed Adam death and instead of being know in the gate they were thrown out of it. She literally got them both evicted and "did not do him good." It appears to me that they ate at a dinner setting due to the fact that Adam was with her when they ate and the Bible doesn't say that she called him over to her. Had she done that, he could have clearly seen where she was getting the food from and refused to eat and could have prevented her from eating. Also had she said to him when ask what was for dinner, today dear we are eating from that forbidden tree. I hear it can make us wise. There is no mention of Adam asking but only receiving what she offered to him. No matter where we can take this argument it is clear that Eve offered this food to Adam. The ability for our husbands to trust that we will do them good all the days of our lives is the the vital element that is required to produce the fragrance the Lord wants. Just like one would choose a vanilla spice candle as the fragrance for their home, TRUST is the fragrance the Lord likes. The bible tells us that the spirit of man is the candle of the Lord in Proverbs 20:27 "The spirit of man is the candle of the Lord, searching all the inward parts of the belly." What lights this candle is the Lord Himself as We die to self. What keeps this wick trimmed is the husband's trust in his wife. For each selfless, sincere sacrifice sends up a sweet smell to God and He comes down in spiritual fire and consumes our sacrifice and fills our spirit. It is the wind of his presence that causes this soothing ambiance to blow softly throughout each room in His house within our hearts.

A Miracle Just for Me

For the Lord God is a sun and shield: the Lord will give grace and glory: no good thing will he withhold from them that walk uprightly (Psalm 84:11)

Now back to my Proverbs 31 handy friend who was with me at the carpet store. God used her to redo my entire house. She befriended me on purpose, she told me—solely because she felt in her spirit that I needed her. All she asked for in return was that I watch her four-month-old son at my house while she worked.

As I was busy perfecting the Lord's house I didn't realize my own house was being redone. One day I looked around and realized everything was new. She even showed me how to paint and to put down ceramic floor tile. We did my new laundry room floor together. I now have new carpet, and every room in the house is repainted. I have a new stair rail, new kitchen cabinets and floor, a new dishwasher, stove and refrigerator. Washer and dryer. New living room furniture with new updated end tables and lamps. New dining room furniture. New windows and a new roof and yes, new curtains. No good thing will He withhold from those who walk uprightly (Psalm 84:11b). Its as if the Lord moved my husband out of the way. I don't even remember talking to him about any of the changes and there was no war.

Chapter 5

A Place Prepared for You

I go to prepare a place for you (John 14:1b)

Finally God placed these verses in my spirit: "Let not your hearts be troubled; ye believe in God, believe also in me. In my Father's house are many mansions. If it were not so, I would have told you. I go to prepare a place for you. And if I go and prepare a place for you I will come again and receive you unto myself; that where I am you may be also" (John 14:1-3).

This verse is often used as a future tense but it is a present day passage. The word "mansions" in this passage according to Strong's Exhaustive Concordance #3306 means "a staying, i.e. residence (the act or the place): abode." Jesus also says, "If a man loves me, he will keep my words; and my Father will love him and we will come unto him and make our abode with him" (John 14:23). Jesus is preparing our mansion just like He said.

However it is through us here and now that this work is being accomplished. Each of us must allow Him to build it and furnish it through us.

Final Thoughts

"Except the Lord build the house, they labour in vain that build it" (Psalm 127:1).

Now that Jesus has completed His house within my heart I am filled with peace, and I can feel His abiding presence within me. He then asked if I noticed that no lights shone throughout the house. I mentioned the light over the dinning room table. He said that that was only on for the purpose of bringing our judging words to light. As I pondered His question He said to me, "Love your husband." I told him that I thought

Chapter 5

that was what I had been learning to do, by perfecting His house within my heart. He told me that I had only set my spirit free. "Now," He said, "you need to love him so the lights in My house can be turned on."

I have begun my new journey with the Lord. My spirit has been set free. Each of us has our own house to prepare. "Ye also, as lively stones, are built up a spiritual house, an holy priesthood, to offer up spiritual sacrifices, acceptable to God by Jesus Christ" (1 Peter 2:5).

And Hebrews 3:6 reads, "But Christ as a son over his own house; whose house are we, if we hold fast the confidence and the rejoicing of the hope firm unto the end."

We cannot prepare anyone else's house. We each have our own walk to walk and our own race to run.

I have joy in my heart. I feel Christ everywhere within me. From the top of my head to the bottom of my feet, He is alive in me. It is a precious gift. My husband did not change, but I have, and all is well with my soul. I am humbled at the thought of my new journey with the Lord as He shows me how to turn the lights on in His house within my heart. When situations arise in which I am tempted to get angry with my husband, Christ in me rises up and keeps me at peace, giving soft answers through me. By my yielding totally to Him, He has full control over His house within my heart.

God is the third person in the marriage covenant and a three-fold cord is not easily broken according to Ecclesiastes 4:12. A Husband and wife alone cannot build the perfect home. We must allow the Lord to build it because He is the Lord of our lives. How wonderful it would be if both couples understood the role they have in building the Lord's place of rest.

"Except the Lord build the house, they labour in vain that build it" (Psalm 127:1).

CPSIA information can be obtained at www.ICGtesting.com
Printed in the USA
LVOW04s1449091114

412755LV00011B/318/P